GROWTH
LEADERSHIP

TRANSFORMATIONAL COMMAND

Developing Growth Leaders in a Time of Crisis

MICHAEL RODGERS

Growth Leadership – Transformational Command
© 2008

Michael D. Rodgers

First edition by BookSurge Publishing
Printed in the United States of America

ISBN: 1-4392-2788-8

To Seth, Nate, Weston, Wesley, Taylor, and Jacob
may the principles and insights contained in this book
help you accomplish your greatest dreams...
to become leaders in your own right.

CONTENTS

FOREWORD

D o we have true leaders today, or are we all followers? In response to our current economic recession and leadership crisis, Michael Rodgers, has created a profound, yet practical guide for both active and aspiring growth leaders. *Growth Leadership – Transformational Command: Developing Growth Leaders in a Time of Crisis* offers a timely model for leaders to be catalysts in their own organizations.

A sign of the times; most recently the Harvard Business Review published its January edition titled *Transforming Leaders.* Tom Rath put out the follow up book to StrengthsFinder 2.0, "Strengths-Based Leadership" and now author Rodgers completes the leadership trend with *Growth Leadership.*

I am pleased that today and tomorrow's leaders will have *Growth Leadership* as a guide by their side! This scholarly book speaks with engaging frankness that helps leaders tackle seemingly insurmountable challenges. Above all, *Growth Leadership* is an inspiring book and timeless read that hits home; imperative reading for every CEO and board member alike.

Derry M. Thompson, Senior Vice President
Graham Corporation – Developing Solutions Building Success

My interest in the nature and function of leadership began early and has continued unabated. From my early scouting days, through my college years, to my current career with Microsoft Corporation, I have closely observed the ways in which effective leadership moves organizations in creative and productive directions and helps all organizational members fulfill their potentials. Continuing to be impressed by leadership examples I see each day, I strive to emulate those leadership models.

Over the past couple of years, I have become especially interested in a growing phenomenon called *growth leadership* and in the characteristics of emerging *growth leaders*. These mid-level manager-leaders, often operating outside formal leadership positions, are combining leadership, management, and entrepreneurial skills in ways that creatively promote organic growth. Their contributions are being increasingly felt, and their influence is steadily growing.

Woodrow Wilson said it best, "You are not here merely to make a living. You are here in order to enable the world to live more amply, with greater vision, with a finer spirit of hope and achievement. You are here to enrich the world, and you impoverish yourself if you forget the errand."

This book is intended to illuminate further the growth leadership movement and to describe some ways in which growth leaders think about themselves and their responsibilities. This book is directed toward leaders and managers (at all organizational levels) who are seeking to draw out leadership potentials in them and in all their people. I hope the observations provided will promote dialogue and discourse around the subject of growth leadership, and I sincerely hope this book will inform and inspire both established and aspiring leaders to live beyond themselves; growth leadership in action.

Michael D. Rodgers

Corporate leadership seen as a "top story" function—a responsibility carried out by highly skilled senior executives. Over the years, we have seen outstanding examples of this top down leadership and we have admired the charismatic and innovative CEOs who have moved their organizations forward.

In recent years, researchers and senior leaders have been training attention on a new kind of leader—the *growth leader*—a mid-level manager who creatively combines managerial skills, leadership talents, and entrepreneurial abilities in ways that achieve surprising results.

In a recent study, researchers Carr, Liedtka, Rosen, and Wiltban (2008) examined the behaviors of fifty of these growth leaders and identified some key qualities:

- All possessed rich and wide experience.
- All possessed great belief in their abilities.
- All thrived on accepting and meeting challenges.
- All possessed a belief in their ability to effect change.
- All seemed capable of changing the rules.
- All possessed the ability to manage risk.
- All preferred people to data.[1]

Many of these growth leaders lie buried within their organizations—their skills and leadership abilities often unnoticed and their potentials for generating organic growth under-recognized and under-utilized.

However, major CEOs are taking note. CEO Jeffrey Immelt at General Electric has instituted changes in the company's famed talent management process—training with special attention on high-potential executives who exhibit growth leadership traits. Others are following suit.

The influence of these emerging growth leaders seems to reflect fundamental changes in the modern business organization. Much of the talk today is about *teams, empowerment,* and *creativity.* Handy (1997) points out that, the key words are *options,* not *plans,* and *possible* rather than the perfect; *involvement* instead of *obedience.* Handy wrote:

> *The new organizations are dispersed. Workers employed in many different offices and locations, wear different hats, and do not necessarily owe all their loyalty to one organization. This has always been true in the political community; now it is also true of the work organization. No longer does everyone have to be in the same place at the same time to get the work done.... More and more, the organization is a 'box of contracts' rather than a lifetime home for all its people.... The leadership of these groups is not of the old-fashioned 'follow me' type. You could call it a distributed leadership.... The leadership in the middle of the organization is a distributed function, often going by other names.[2]*

In the chapters that follow, Michael further defines the nature of growth leadership and the special characteristics of these mid-level growth leaders. Michael addresses a few important questions:

- What kinds of specific behaviors, traits, attitudes, beliefs, and values characterize growth leaders?

- How do growth leaders think about themselves, and how do they achieve their objectives within the strictures of conventional organizational life?

- What kinds of thinking skills do growth leaders deploy in their daily leadership activities?

- How do they harness the energy of their teams and move them toward desired visions and outcomes?

Michael hope's the information will train even more attention on the role of the growth leader and the potentials for tapping into this type of leadership style as a valuable resource. In addition, I hope the discussions will stimulate further dialogue around the growth leadership phenomenon.

Orlo Otteson

CHAPTER ONE

GROWTH LEADERSHIP AND CREATIVE THINKING

Amerian business success, and corporate success around the world, rests heavily on creative and innovative approaches to problems and opportunities. In a hypercompetitive and knowledge-rich global economy, creative leadership lies at the heart of successful business enterprises. However, what do we mean by *creativity?* What are the core elements of *creative leadership,* and what is its relation to growth leadership?

This interest in creativity—the generation of new ideas and the translation of those ideas into action—has evolved over the years. One icon of twentieth-century industry, John D. Rockefeller, once dismissed innovative work with these words: "I have never felt the need for scientific knowledge, have never felt it. A young man who wants to succeed in business does not require chemistry or physics. He can always hire scientists."[3]

I now see more clearly the need for creative leadership, and we are seeing the ways in which creativity and creative leadership can enhance organizational performance—at all levels of corporate life. In the words of Florida (2002), an economist at Carnegie Mellon University:

> *We are embarking on an age of pervasive creativity that permeates all sectors of the economy and society—not just seeing bursts of innovation from high-tech industries. We are truly in the midst of a creative transformation with the onset of a Creative Economy.*[4]

Creativity and creative thinking

In recent years, various researchers and scholars have linked the concepts of *change* and *leadership*, and have developed a topic they call (unsurprisingly) *change leadership.* Many of these investigators have long understood the connections between effective leadership and required change activities. However, many seem to have skipped past a key element—that is, the nature and function of *creativity*, a uniquely human characteristic that allows us to imagine and create new worlds.

The term *creativity* defined in various ways, but it generally refers to the ways in which an individual, using diverse modes of thought, generates new ideas and solutions. The tangled process for getting there, however, can prove complex. The famed psychologist, William James (1995), writing in 1880, grasped the ideational complexities surrounding divergent thinking:

> *Instead of thoughts of concrete things patiently following one another in a beaten track of habitual suggestion, we have the most abrupt cross-cuts and transitions from one idea to another...the most unheard of combinations of elements, the subtle associations of analogy; in a word, we seem suddenly introduced into a seething caldron of ideas...where partnerships can be joined or loosened in an instant, treadmill routine is unknown, and the unexpected seems the only law.*[5]

Many growth leaders—mid-managers who consistently apply creative thinking to organizational problems and opportunities—often operate outside the boundaries of a formal leadership position. In fact, many of these creative leaders might be inclined to say, "But I'm not a leader. I've not assumed a leadership position." Leaders are influencing others often and effectively moving their teams in creative and productive directions.

Creative leadership

The term *leadership* defies precise definition, but instead viewed as a *process* intended to produce *change*. In this sense, it diverges from the basic function of *management*—a process intended to produce *consistent outcomes*.

Managers strive to develop efficient processes and routines. Transformational leaders strive to create new ideas, policies, and procedures. Organizations need both capabilities, and the two functions often overlap. Growth leaders, many of them mid-managers, frequently find themselves in both roles—managing teams while leading them toward new and innovative goals.

Approaches vary. Some growth leaders accept existing paradigms, but find ways to extend them. Others reject existing paradigms and try to replace them. Still others integrate existing paradigms and form new ones.

In all cases, however, creative leaders develop original ideas that *serve some purpose.* They develop new ideas and practices that go beyond simple novelty or originality—*ones that lead to new and useful products and services.* These products (tangible and intangible) are usually original and novel, but they also *meet a need.*

The creative leader's contributions transcend customs, traditions, and habitual ways of thinking. His or her ideas counter arguments such as "But that's our policy" or "That's just the way we do things around here." William James (1995) noted the restrictive and stifling effect of habit:

> *The force of habit, the grip of convention hold us down on the Trivial Plane; we are unaware of our bondage because the bonds are invisible, the restraints acting below the level of awareness. They are the collective standards of value, codes of behaviour, matrices with built in axioms which determine the rules of the game, and make most of us run, most of the time, in the grooves of habit—reducing us to the status of skilled automata which Behaviorism proclaims to be the only condition of man.*[6]

Years later, Gestalt psychologists defined the differences between *reproductive* and *productive* thought. Reproductive thinkers, in their view, look to previously successful behaviors. They stay stuck in old thought habits—unwilling or unable to deal with novelty. Productive or insightful thinkers, however, use past experience at a general level—while dealing with each new problem or opportunity on its own terms. They engage in divergent thinking, refusing to become fixated or trapped. They do not attempt to apply specific knowledge to *irrelevant* problems or issues. They break out of scripts and the boundaries set by established knowledge. No longer skilled automata, they respond to environmental changes in imaginative and novel ways.

Creative change: a systems model

Persons. Various researchers over the years have trained attention on leadership traits and characteristics on the *person.* They have examined the individual skills, attributes, and motivations that influence creative leadership actions. Moreover, they have identified some specific creative leader characteristics:

- *Creative leaders challenge the process.* They look for innovative ways to improve the organization. They search for opportunities. They experiment and take risks.

- *Creative leaders inspire a shared vision.* They create an ideal image of what the organization (or some part of it) might become. They envision the future and enlist others.

- *Creative leaders motivate and enable others.* They build spirited teams. They foster collaboration and strengthen others.

- *Creative leaders model the way.* They insist on humane treatment of others. They show how goals should be pursued.

- *Creative leaders encourage the heart.* They make their people feel like heroes. They recognize contributions and celebrate accomplishments.[7]

Researchers Carr and others (2008) note that growth leaders possess a deep-seated belief in their abilities and in their power to shape the world around them. Confident growth leaders often skirt authority and find ways to work around imposed goals. They sometimes "break the rules," but they avoid actions that undermine organizational well-being. They possess sound social, emotional, moral, and cultural intelligences; and they rely strongly on self-management and self-evaluation skills.[8]

Growth leaders believe in their abilities for good reasons. They have learned how to identify and use their strengths, while mitigating their weaknesses; they are strongly guided by inner goals and standards. They accept challenges and persist in the face of failure. They are mainly interested in meeting their goals and less interested in outperforming or "defeating" others. They thrive on challenges, but they establish realistic goals and strive to minimize risks. They seem to possess a quality the late scholar David McClelland called *achievement motivation.*

Process. Researchers Puccio, Murdock, and Mance (2007) point out that creative change (while beginning with an individual or a team of individuals) rests heavily on the presence of a *process*—on the stages of thinking that go into opportunity-seeking or problem-solving approaches. The quality of this process directly influences the quality of the product or service, and both influenced by ways in which individuals express their creativity. Michael Kirton (1999) has identified two creative styles:

- An *adaptive* orientation (creating through continuous improvement of existing ideas and systems)

- An *innovative* orientation (creating by introducing radically new ideas that challenge the existing routines, processes, and policies).[9]

Both approaches can foster high levels of creativity, and organizations need both approaches—they need a balance between *continuous* and *discontinuous* change.

Moreover, individuals interact with the creative process in differing ways. As the process unfolds, some will find certain parts easier to deal with than others will—some will simply find certain parts more interesting. Creative leaders understand how to establish, evaluate, and manage the creative process. They understand the differences between *clarifiers, ideators, developers*, and *implementers*. Furthermore, they understand the ways in which each type relates to the creative process. Growth leaders respect individual differences and preferences, while maintaining the ability to resolve conflicts and clashes—they know how to keep the process moving.

Environment. The presence of creative leaders and processes will foster innovation, but it will not guarantee creative change. People and processes do not operate in a vacuum. They operate in a specific *environment*—in an organizational *climate* and *culture*. This organizational climate (a powerful influence) seen as the recurrent patterns of behavior, attitudes, and feelings that characterize organizational life. It differs from corporate *culture*—the patterns of basic assumptions, values, beliefs, symbols, and meanings that define behavioral standards, norms, and expectations.

Culture rests on deep-rooted assumptions, and it remains stable over time. Climate, a manifestation of culture, is more changeable and more easily influenced by leadership style. Harvard business professor Teresa Amabile (1988) has identified some key factors that both help and hinder workplace creativity:

- *Stimulants*

Freedom	Recognition
Effective project management	Sufficient time
Adequate resources	Sufficient challenge
Collaborative atmosphere	

11

- *Obstacles*

Too much bureaucracy	Insufficient resources
Inappropriate rewards	Time pressure
Lack of cooperation	Need to maintain the status quo.[10]
Organizational disinterest	

Amabile's research shows that "regular people" can demonstrate impressive leadership abilities. Creative leadership talent is not the exclusive property of a few "high creative" types—a talent handed down from on high.

Moreover, creative change occurs when a creative product (tangible or intangible) is *adopted*, when the innovative idea has been *implemented*. These products develop most effectively when the three creative elements (*person*, *process*, and *environment*) are interacting in a balanced fashion.

Growth leadership (and transformational leadership in general) fosters and promotes creativity. Northouse (2004) puts it this way:

> *Transformational leadership] includes leadership that stimulates followers to be creative and innovative, and to challenge their own beliefs and values as well as those of the leader and the organization. This type of leadership supports followers as they try new approaches and develop innovative ways of dealing with organizational issues. It promotes followers' thinking things out on their own and engaging in careful problem solving.[11]*

Creativity, a core leadership competence, is a process that leads to *positive* change. Today's complex business climate requires (indeed demands) leaders who embody creativity and who can facilitate the creative talents of others. As quoted by Simonton (1984), "…when the most famous creators and leaders are under scrutiny, the distinction between creativity and leadership vanishes, because creativity becomes a form of leadership."[12]

Creativity can drive an organization powerfully; but time pressure, fear, and competition can hinder progress. In addition, researchers tell us that financial reward and organizational streamlining often have little effect on creative thinking.

Creative leaders initiate fresh and untested approaches. They persistently seek potential opportunities. They stay proactive. They tolerate chaos and ambiguity. They avoid premature closure. They avoid traps and fixations. Additionally, they strive always to maintain a creative organizational climate and culture.

Growth leaders, often operating in relative obscurity, provide solid examples of creative thinking and energizing actions on a regular basis. They show the ways in which all organizational members can tap into their creative capital. Furthermore, they inspire and manage change—while helping others develop their own leadership potentials. In the words of management educator Charles Handy (1993), "We cannot wait for great visions from great people, for they are in short supply.... It is up to us to light our own small fires in the darkness."[13]

CHAPTER TWO

GROWTH LEADERSHIP
AND VISIONARY THINKING

Growth leaders, creative and forward-thinking mid-managers, exhibit a kind of *visionary thinking* on a daily basis—a keen ability to imagine and articulate a desired future. A clear and compelling vision sets a direction and identifies goals—it inspires, energizes, and organizes team members. Researchers Bennis and Nanus (1985) put it well:

> *When an organization has a clear sense of its purpose, direction, and desired future state, and when this image is widely shared, individuals are able to find their own roles both in the organization and in the larger society of which they are a part. This empowers individuals and confers status upon them because they can see themselves as part of a worthwhile enterprise. They gain a sense of importance, as they are transformed from robots blindly following instructions to human beings engaged in a creative and purposeful venture. Individuals in a team without a vision are likely to become disengaged and frustrated.*[14]

Vision-creating skills lie at the core of growth leadership. A compelling vision unifies and drives creativity; it creates a bridge between the present and the future. A vision can take various forms. It might be a roughly formed notion that researchers Collins and Porras (1994) call a *Big Hairy Audacious Idea*.[15] Alternatively, it might be just a fresh view of how a team or a process should (or could) operate more effectively. In all cases, the vision projects a clear and vivid image of a *desired future*. It creates a lens through which organizational members can focus their creative efforts and activities.

Effective *visionary thinking* begins with some effective *diagnostic* thinking, the ability to assess circumstances, define problems, and then lay out creative pathways to change. Diagnostic thinking, driven by sound data management, helps leaders establish a realistic vision and adapt to shifting circumstances. In short, it helps them "make sense" of the potentials for resolving a problem or seizing an opportunity.

Sensemaking, closely tied to diagnostic and visionary thinking, defined as the ability or attempt to understand and make sense of an ambiguous, complex, and uncertain situation. Growth leaders possess the ability to understand the context in which the organization (and its people) operates. They keep a close eye on the environment, while simultaneously instituting change, and they constantly strive to "make sense" of a fast-moving, high-tech world.

Sensemakers rely heavily on *data*, but they define the term *data* rather broadly. These leaders cast a wide information gathering net. They use all available data collection tools, and they rely on hard facts. However, in their early assessments, they also use observations, hunches, guesses, hypotheses, and even feelings. They try to spot incongruities and information gaps, and they often look to people (rather than raw market data) for insights and guidance.

Divergent and convergent thinking

In their book, *Creative Leadership: Skills That Drive Change*, researchers Puccio, Murdock, and Mance urge leaders to use both *divergent* and *convergent* thinking tools in their diagnostic and visionary efforts. Divergent thinking is to generate many ideas, brainstorming, by questions, including those used by good journalists: *Who, What, Where, When, Why.*

- **Who:** Who is involved? Who is the primary decision maker? Who are all the people affected by this situation?

- **What:** What is the history behind this situation? What is the ideal outcome? What's already been tried?

- **When:** When did this start? When would you like to take action? When would you like to have this resolved?

- **Where:** Where is this taking place? Where in the situation been successfully managed and how is it been managed? Where can one find similar situations and how are they similar?

- **Why:** Why is the situation important? Why is it occurring? Why are you, or others, concerned about it?[16]

In divergent thinking, team members go for quantity. They make connections and come at problems from all angles. They also keep posing, the why?

- Why is this happening?

- Why is it a problem?

- Why is it important?

When they have formulated initial answers to all the "Why" questions, divergent thinkers start over—applying the "Why" question once more to each answer, digging even deeper. When all is been laid out, divergent thinkers creative side then moves to the next step—*convergent thinking*. This process helps sort out the "dreams" and goals that seem most worthy.

Researchers Treffinger, Isaksen, and Firestien (1982) recommend some specific convergent thinking tools, including the use of "hits" and "highlighting." In this approach, participants simply review the hits (the list of options) and highlight those that jump out or that seem most relevant. Choices can be based on simple intuition—they do not have to be justified. Team members then move the hits into clusters—groups of options that have some similarity—and they name each cluster, using a word or phrase that captures its meaning. They then form a consensus decision about where next to go in the creative process.[17]

This problem-solving process is described in detail by authors Puccio, Murdock, and Mance.[18] It can, over time, help develop and sharpen visionary thinking skills. It can help team members create an image of a desired outcome and future.

Critical thinking skills are in play throughout the entire diagnostic and visioning process. Good thinking, traditionally, has been seen in terms of cognitive ability. However, researchers in the Cognitive Skills Group at Project Zero (Harvard University) have proposed a new view of what it means to be a good thinker. These researchers have identified seven broad patterns that are central to high-level thinking and that seem to apply directly to visionary thinking and leadership in general:

- The disposition to be broad and adventurous

- The disposition to wonder, to identify problems, to investigate

- The disposition to build explanations and understandings

- The disposition to make plans and to be strategic

- The disposition to be intellectually careful and precise

- The disposition to ask for and evaluate reasons

- The disposition to be metacognitive (to think about the "thinking" process)

We all possess abilities that we fail to use, rarely use, or insufficiently use, yet we seldom suffer serious consequences. However, when leaders possess specific abilities and are not *disposed* to use them, they fall short of their potentials, and they fail their followers. Growth leaders show us that it is not enough to possess good critical and creative thinking skills. Leaders must also possess *critical thinking dispositions*—they must possess the three psychological components that spark *dispositional behavior*:

- *Ability*—the basic capacity to carry out a behavior

- *Inclination*—the motivation to engage in a behavior

- *Sensitivity*—the ability to see the appropriateness of a behavior

One overarching thinking disposition seems to stand out; that is, good thinkers show a tendency toward "mindfulness." These mindful thinkers tend to create new categories—or simply "pay attention" to given contexts. They stay open to new information, and they tend to examine various perspectives.

Others have noted that mindful thinkers maintain a positive attitude toward ambiguous and complex situations. They possess intellectual humility, courage, integrity, and perseverance. Furthermore, they display open-mindedness, inquisitiveness, self-confidence, and maturity. All these traits and attributes (and there are others) seem also to characterize the growth leader.

Visionary thinking and values

Visionary thinking, closely tied to a leader's individual *values* and to the organization's overall *value system*. A desired future—a clear vision—rests heavily on the *ends* one wants to achieve and the *means* one chooses to attain them. Our actions mainly bespeak our values. However, what are values? Moreover, what is their relation to visionary thinking?

Our behavior (both individual and organizational) is influenced by specific personal preferences (needs and desires), specific prescriptions for behavior (shoulds and oughts), general preferences (likes and interests), and general philosophies (morals and ethics).

It is our *values* that mainly guide our ongoing activities and our *conceptions of the desirable*—both the desirable *end-states of existence* we wish to achieve (growth, creativity) and the preferred *modes-of-conduct* (honesty, competence) we choose to achieve them. Values tell us what is right, good, and desirable; and they help us evaluate the morality of our behavior and the degree of our competence. Moreover, *value-focused thinking*—the ability to recognize and articulate essential values—lies at the heart of visionary thinking.

A value possesses a *content* attribute and an *intensity* attribute. We identify specific values, but we also assign importance to each. We organize our values into a *value hierarchy* that helps us choose between and among possible courses of action. We weigh our individual, organizational, and societal values against one another and rank them. We prioritize our values and order them into a value system—a value hierarchy. This hierarchical concept helps us understand that individuals, organizations, and societies can and seen not only in terms of specific values, but also in terms of their value *priorities*.

A value system develops bit by bit over time. It's intricately interwoven with habitual conduct as well as with a more cognitive decision-making activities. The value system is a comprehensive mental structure and matrix that we never fully activate at any one time. We consult the most immediately relevant part and ignore, for the moment, the rest. We activate different subsets of the system according to the circumstances in which we find ourselves and according to the ways in which we have ranked our individual, organizational, and societal values.

The total value system remains sufficiently stable over time to provide us with some sense of continuity and meaning. However, the system also retains the flexibility required to rearrange the hierarchy as changes occur in our individual and organizational lives. Thus, a value system maintains its enduring and stable nature while also preserving its fluid and dynamic qualities.

We reorder our values slowly and reluctantly, but we can and do reorder them. If our values were completely stable, individual and organizational change would come too slowly—if at all. If they were completely unstable, we would fail to achieve order and continuity in organizational and human affairs.

Moreover, values are also rooted in our thinking styles—in the ways we arrive at "truth." Hunter Lewis (1990) has identified six of these thinking styles:

- *Authority*: We take someone else's word (our parents, for example) or we place our faith in an external authority such as the state. ("I trust the authority of....")

- *Deductive logic*: We subject our beliefs to deductive reasoning. ("Since A is true, B must be true.")

- *Sense experience*: We gain direct knowledge through our senses. ("I know this is true because I saw it, I heard it, I smelled it, or I touched it.")

- *Emotion*: We feel that something is right, and we use our feelings to make judgments. ("I feel in my heart that this is true.")

- *Intuition*: We use our unconscious-intuitive mind to derive insights and problem solutions. ("When I awoke this morning, the solution came to me in a flash.")

- *Science*: We use sense experience to collect the observable facts, intuition to develop a testable hypothesis about the facts, logic to develop the experiment, and sense experience again to complete the test. ("I tested the hypothesis experimentally and found that it was true.")[19]

We seldom focus consciously on these six modes of reasoning, but the main point seems clear. Our values are closely related, not only to deeply rooted traditions but also to the ways in which we arrive at them. By adopting and emphasizing one tradition or thinking style over another, we transform it into a dominant personal or social value that colors all other value choices.

Moreover, in the construction of our value system, we usually call on a combination of traditions and thinking styles—each with a different emphasis. That combination is one of the reasons why human and social values are so subtle, complex, and diverse—and one of several reasons why they are so complicated.

A compelling vision, then, seems directly related to a clear understanding of organizational values and their relation to individual values. A good vision statement can begin with the formulation of a good values statement—both can grow out of the divergent and convergent thinking process. Examples abound while a vivid image of a desired future—a vision—sends a powerful message. In the words of Kouzes and Posner (1995):

> *Envisioning the future begins with a vague desire to do something that would challenge yourself and others. As the desire grows in intensity so does your determination. The strength of this internal energy forces you to clarify what it is that you really want to do. You begin to get a sense of what you want the organization to look like and be like when you and others have completed the journey.*[20]

Effective visions and sound values drive creativity and innovation, and both lie at the heart of effective growth leadership—as does the ability to *dream* and to imagine a future that might be years away.

Effective dreaming, supported by specific vision-setting skills and sound dispositional thinking, strongly guides the creative thinking process and powerfully guides the growth leader's activities.

CHAPTER THREE

GROWTH LEADERSHIP AND STRATEGIC-TACTICAL THINKING

Strategic thinking

Growth leaders, highly productive mid-managers, create compelling visions while developing creative pathways for reaching that vision. The process of laying out the steps in that pathway is called *strategic thinking*—a focused activity that identifies critical issues and potential opportunities.

Strategic thinkers build bridges to the future. They move organizational thinking from vision creation (a good start) to concrete planning efforts and then to descriptions of the ideas and actions that may (or will) move the company forward. Without effective strategic thinking, companies risk falling into the Christopher Columbus School of Management:

- When he left—he did not know where he was going.

- When he got there—he did not know where he was.

- When he returned—he could not tell where he had been.

The nature of strategic thinking has evolved over the years, moving from an emphasis on analysis and planning to a more entrepreneurial, opportunistic approach. In today's dynamic, hypercompetitive business world, companies (and units within companies) can quickly get outflanked. Effective strategic thinkers must keep an extremely close eye on the environment—monitoring their markets, assessing their competition, and examining emerging trends— while simultaneously setting critical directions. It all adds up to a formidable challenge and the need for an effective set of strategic and tactical thinking tools.

Problem finding

Much strategic thinking focuses on *problem solving*—a function that begins with *problem-finding* and *problem-defining* activities. Some managers and leaders might say, "But why do we have to *find* problems? We seem to have our full share." Nonetheless, business scholars and other analysts have long understood the need for a deliberate approach to problem-finding, defined by Jay and Perkins (1997) as "…behaviors, attitudes, and thought processes that are directed toward the *envisionment,* posing, formulation, and creation of problems, as opposed to the process involved in solving them."[21]

Why the need to find problems in a business environment that seems laden with tribulations and challenges? Additionally, what is the relation of problem-finding and problem-definition to strategic thinking?

The problem-finding process—a critical first step in an ongoing circular creative process—strives to overcome some initial problem-solving obstacles including the initial resistance to new ideas. When confronted with a new concept or approach, team members often (not always) rush to judgment. They too quickly move into an overly critical stance, prematurely shutting down the flow of productive thinking. They understandably wish to be considered "practical" in their approach and "logical" in their thinking. Instead of staying open to new approaches—and finding ways to shape promising but imperfect ideas—they often reach instead for familiar and available solutions.

The result? Decisions are becoming directed toward a single goal—even though most problems involve multiple goals. Creative attitudes, behaviors, and skills stay underdeveloped and strategic thinking stalls or stops.

This resistance to new ideas and tendency toward early and hasty evaluation thwarts the need for deeper inquiries and sounder understandings. However, the resistance is understandable. Over the years, we have tended to admire decisive and fast-moving leaders and managers. We have tended to suspect those who creatively explore gray areas and fine distinctions. We have too often focused on problem-*solutions* rather than problem-*definitions,* and too often we have failed to find a balance between our urge to narrow a problem (thus missing the "big picture") and our urge to broaden a problem (thus failing to break it into manageable pieces).

Moreover, many organizational members (some with careers in mind) fear potential failure and the accompanying criticism. The need to "belong" and to follow familiar paths can outweigh the need for bold and risky thinking. Inquisitiveness and curiosity can go unrewarded, and often can be equated with foolish and unrealistic expectations. No one wishes considered a "fool" or a "dreamer." Thus, group-think can dominate discussions and thwart needed imaginative probings and explorations. Important questions while buried. Problems can go unresolved and opportunities unrealized. Moreover, strategic thinking stopped in its tracks.

Creative leaders and creative strategic thinkers, however, are not without resources. Creative leadership and solid strategic thinking can clear away resistance, while spurring progress toward a desired goal. Creative leaders can develop tools and resources that engage team members in a proactive, forward looking, and strategically productive process. Many growth leaders (many of them operating outside a formal leadership position) have provided outstanding strategic thinking examples. So, what are some of these broad talents?

First, creative leaders and all strategic thinkers exhibit their commitment to the creative process on a regular basis. They get involved, and they pick up their end—they avoid the temptation simply to dump challenges on others. They develop tactics and methods that promote imaginative, innovative, and productive strategies. They show the way—they *model* the desired behavior.

Second, these leaders set up structures that help employees generate, advance, and implement new ideas. They show how tactical challenges align with strategic goals, and they manage their people and teams in an orderly but fluid fashion. They develop a common language that facilitates communication and interaction, and they establish a set of *divergent thinking* tools that opens up thinking, spurs creative problem-solving, and promotes adaptability. Let us look at a few.

Statement starters

The ways in which one frames a question influences the response. Well-framed questions drive thinking into deeper levels and toward a more creative domain. Open-ended questions free up the strategic thinking processes and generate ideas.

These questions prompt participants to move from a negative to a positive stance—to richer possibility thinking. Changing key words within the problem-solving statement can also precipitate new thought combinations and patterns. The use of *statement starters* helps frame thinking and identifies challenges. Wish fulfillment language also helps:

- Wouldn't it be nice (or cool) if…?

- I wish we….

- What I would really like to see is….

After formulating these starter statements, team members can then pose some questions:

- **Why**

  Why is this occurring?

  Why is it important?

  Why can we not afford to ignore it?

- **Where**

  Where is this occurring?

  Where are there similar situations?

  Where has it been successfully managed?

- **When**

  When did this start?

  When should we take action?

  When would we like to have it resolved?

- **Who**

  Who is involved?

  Who is the primary decision maker?

  Who is affected by the situation?

- **What**

  What keeps us from getting past this?

  What will we lose if we don't do anything?

  What resources do we have?

After answering these questions, team members can evaluate the relevance of the information and assign grades to each item within a set of answers—an exercise in convergent thinking (narrowing the options).

- H = high relevance

- M = medium relevance

- L = low relevance

Problem-finding and problem-definition require the ability to tolerate ambiguity and to manage unresolved tension—to wait patiently as options and potential solutions come into view. Both activities—problem-finding and problem-defining—lead ultimately to *solution-finding* and *acceptance-finding.*

Solution finding

Problem-finding managers and leaders move finally to a *solution-finding* phase, a stage in which they filter potential solutions through important criteria. They must then engage in *evaluative thinking.* They must consider the worth of their ideas and the workability of their proposed actions. They must generate some *action steps*—concrete, observable activities that lead to a desired outcome. In short, they must engage in *tactical thinking.*

Evaluative thinking helps determine the kinds of ideas that should move forward and the criteria through which they should move. Evaluative thinking allows a certain pause in the activities—a period of reflection that slows the rush toward implementation and permits team members to scan the environment into which they are introducing their solution or change. This pause permits participants to assess the people, resources, and conditions that will either advance or thwart the new idea.

Brainstorming is helpful in this phase, but researchers Puccio, Murdock, and Mance (2007) recommend a tool they call *Pluses, Potentials, Concerns, and*

Overcoming Concerns.[22] This process, they say, keeps novelty alive, since it requires two rounds of affirmative evaluation before participants look at the concerns and the potential roadblocks.

In the first two steps (*Pluses* and *Potentials*), team members list as many "positives" as they can, using divergent thinking guidelines.

They then phrase *Concerns* in the form of a challenge statement, using statement starters such as:

- How can…?

- How might…?

- What might…?

This step invites ideas that may strengthen the original idea.

In the fourth step (*Overcoming Concerns*), participants generate ideas they think will overcome the most *important* concerns. If a concern cannot be overcome, participants can either go with the original, established idea or drop the new idea altogether and search for an alternative.

At this stage, team members need to begin taking into account the all-important influence of ecology—the intertwining network of conditions, forces, and factors (internal and external) that impinge on the circumstances. If proposed solutions hold up in the face of deliberate evaluation, members can then begin to look at ways of accepting those solutions and passing those solutions on. If not, they may have to revisit the *idea generation* phase. If they *are* able to move directly to the action phase, they must define the outcomes that mark progress toward the goal.

Acceptance finding

In the acceptance-finding phase, problem solvers turn ideas into realities—they shift from thought to action. This implementation stage involves four separate but interrelated actions:

- *Envision the completed project.* Envision the end, and then look back and consider paths traveled. This perceptual shift provides a different vantage point and set of mental patterns. Furthermore, it may prompt new images, ideas, thoughts, and insights.

- *Brainstorm a list of events (or actions) required to complete the project.* Make a list, but do not strive for a logical, sequential order.

- *Plan the events.* After listing the needed events, cluster them in natural groupings. This clustering may reveal actions that can occur simultaneously.

- *Enhance the probability of success.* Ask important questions. What are the benefits derived, and what is the most important benefit? In what ways will the plan benefit people? Who will benefit most? What are the costs and disadvantages of the status quo? What current values need to be maintained or enhanced? Who are the champions and detractors?

Tactical thinking involves an ability to devise a plan that includes specific and measurable steps for attaining a desired end and that also includes methods for measuring progress toward that end. This continuous monitoring reveals the need for course corrections or for further problem solving efforts.

Growth leaders, those highly productive but often under-recognized mid-managers, give us examples of creative thinking —both strategic and tactical. These bottom-up parsing efforts frequently exceed and outperform the "top story" attention grabbing attempts to instill a creative climate. In addition, the creative, action-based processes often prove more productive than the traditional analytical methods.

Growth leaders operate imaginatively and creatively, while avoiding high-risk actions. They place small bets and then study the results. Flying under the corporate radar, they launch small initiatives that, when successful, be enhanced and enlarged. They establish a creative climate that spurs people to think in new ways, which helps them follow a synchronized innovative thinking process.

Creative strategic and tactical thinking is no longer a *choice*. In a fast-moving, highly complex business environment, it is an *imperative*. Growth leaders are showing us imaginative ways to think about problems and opportunities— and to inspire their teams—while developing concrete, rational, and comprehensible steps for reaching desired goals.

CHAPTER FOUR

GROWTH LEADERSHIP
AND ORGANIZATIONAL LIFE

Growth leaders, mid-managers who achieve surprising and impressive results, often operate outside the boundaries of a formal leadership role. Yet, they demonstrate great ability to gather available company resources and apply them in inventive and productive ways. What do these leaders understand about organizational life? Why do they succeed so well when others (with far more authority) stay mired in mediocrity? Moreover, what can we learn from their leadership styles?

Leadership defined as the art of moving people toward a goal. (Harry Truman defined it as "…making people do what they don't want to do, and liking it.") *Management*, a responsibility conferred from above, is defined the efficient and effective integration of resources to achieve goals.

All managers lead to some degree or another, and all leaders manage in one way or another. Growth leaders seem especially able to combine two forms of leadership—*transactional* and *transformational*.

Transactional leadership

Transactional leaders excel at management functions, and they almost always occupy administrative positions within the organization's formal structure. Functioning primarily as managers, these leaders create clear structures and firm expectations, and they establish a well-understood "reward-punishment" system.

Under this system, employees assume full responsibility for carrying out assigned tasks, regardless of their capabilities and their access to needed resources. When they succeed, rewarded, when they fail, are punished. These punishments are not always stated, but well understood, and the organization usually has a formal discipline system in place to mete out the so-called "punishments."

Transactional leaders tend to follow the principle "if it ain't broke, don't fix it"—otherwise called *management by exception*. That is, if a process or function is meeting defined expectations, it is not seen as needing (or deserving) attention.

Transformational leadership

Transformational leadership, a privilege conferred from below, rests on the ability of the leader to persuade, inspire, and inform others in ways that move them toward (and beyond) expected performance levels. Peters and Waterman (1984), in their book, *In Search of Excellence*, define the transformational leader this way:

> *The transforming leader is concerned with minutiae, but he is concerned with a different kind of minutiae; he is concerned with the tricks of the pedagogue, the mentor, the linguist—the more successfully to become the value shaper, the exemplar, the maker of meanings. His job is much tougher than that of the transactional leader, for he is the true artist, the true pathfinder. After all, he is both calling forth and exemplifying the urge for transcendence that unites us all. At the same time, he exhibits almost boorish consistency over long periods of time in support of his one or two transcending values. No opportunity is too small, no forum too insignificant, no audience too junior.*[23]

Transformational leaders set visions and take risks. They serve as catalytic change agents, training attention on new outcomes and fostering creative problem-solving approaches. They motivate team members to look beyond their individual interests—for the sake of the organization. These leaders represent the group, presumed to embody the group's *values*. Phillip Selznick (1982), in his book, *Leadership and Administration*, says this about transformational leadership:

> *The inbuilding of purpose is a challenge to creativity, because it involves transforming individuals and groups from neutral, technical units into participants who have a particular stamp, sensitivity, and commitment. This is ultimately an educational process. It has been well said that the effective leader must know the meaning and master the technique of the educator.... The art of the creative leader is the art of institution building, the reworking of human and technological materials to fashion an organism that embodies new and enduring values.... To institutionalize is to infuse*

with value beyond the technical requirements of the task at hand. The prizing of social machinery beyond its technical role is largely a reflection of the unique way it fulfills personal or group needs. Whenever individuals become attached to an organization or a way of doing things as persons rather than as technicians, the result is a prizing of the device for its own sake. From the standpoint of the committed person, the organization is changed from an expendable tool into a valued source of personal satisfaction.... The institutional leader, then, is primarily an expert in the promotion and protection of values.[24]

Transformational leaders (including growth leaders) understand the nature and uses of values—and the ways in which values shape organizational culture. Growth leaders—transformers all—seem also to understand (either consciously or intuitively) the nature and uses of *power* and *organizational politics*—and they make effective use of both. However, what do we mean by *power*? What are its sources? What is the meaning of organizational *politics*? How does it work, and what is its relation to growth leadership activities?

Leadership power

Power as defined as the *potential* of one individual or group (the agent) to affect the behavior of another (the actor). Power influences who gets what, when, and how. It is viewed as *politics in action.*

In American society, the term *power* is loaded with negative connotations. Individuals who pursue power, or who express interest in acquiring power, are often called *power hungry*—a highly pejorative label. However, power is a means, not an end. As such, used for rational or irrational ends, for benevolent or malicious purposes.

We tend to equate power with only one form—*coercive power*—a type we often associate with authoritarian, dictatorial managers and leaders. Growth leaders, change agents who generally operate outside formal leadership positions, often lack strong coercive power. That is not to say they lack power. Indeed, most are in full possession of several other power sources—leadership tools that move teams forward.

The work of French and Raven (1960) often cited in discussions about power. Building on their work, Hersey, Blanchard, and Natemeyer (1982) have defined seven sources of leadership power:

- **Coercive power** is based on the perception that an individual has the authority to punish or recommend punishment. Its base is fear and the power to criticize, demote, fire, reprimand, and influence financial compensation.

- **Reward power**, the opposite of coercive power, is based on the perception that an individual can provide important formal rewards such as pay increases and promotions and more subjective rewards, such as praise, attention, and recognition.

- **Legitimate power** is based on the perception that an individual has a formal position in the organization and the right to influence by virtue of position or role.

- **Referent power** (or charismatic power) is based on respect and admiration for the leader and a desire to emulate him or her.

- **Expert power** is based on the perception that an individual has the skill, knowledge, and expertise that can facilitate the achievement of another individual's goals.

- **Information power** is based on the perception that an individual either possesses or has access to valuable information that can promote one's interests.

- **Connection power** is based on the perception that an individual has access to powerful persons or groups.[25]

Legitimate power and *referent* power (charismatic power) have less effect on performance. In addition, *reward* power and *coercive* power can, in some instances, negatively affect performance. Simply put, the reward-punishment system does not seem to work very well.

Knowledge, say the experts, is the transformational leader's most effective "power tool" and resource. *Competence*, the *application* of knowledge, appeals to a wide variety of individuals and shown to raise performance levels significantly. In their creative efforts, growth leaders reach across company boundaries and assemble resources in imaginative ways. They put their entrepreneurial skills to work in complex corporate environments. They place people in positions that optimize their strengths, and they are quick to remove them when required. At times, they skirt bureaucratic interference, but they avoid conflict with the organization—they save their fight for the marketplace. They motivate and inspire their people while simultaneously conducting themselves in a tough-minded (but fair) fashion.

While performing these various functions and maneuvers, growth leaders bring into play an array of power sources and tactics—although not always recognized as such:

- **Reason:** the use of facts and data to make a logical or rational presentation of ideas

- **Friendliness:** the use of positive reinforcement, goodwill, humility, and friendliness when making a request

- **Coalition building:** the use of others' support to back up the request

- **Bargaining:** the use of negotiation through the exchange of benefits

- **Assertiveness:** the use of a direct and forceful approach, demands for compliance with requests, reminders about the need to comply with rules and orders

- **Appeals to higher authority:** the use of individuals higher in the organization to back up requests

- **Sanctions:** the use of organizationally derived rewards and punishments such as the withholding or granting of a salary increase, the threat of an unsatisfactory performance evaluation, the threat to withhold a promotion[26]

Researchers have found that individuals do not rely on the seven types of power as being equal in measure. The use of reason, however, is the most popular strategy, regardless of whether the influence is directed upward or downward.

Carr and others (2008) noted that growth leaders combine two seemingly opposing forces: 1) ruthlessly holding people accountable for results and 2) engaging their passion to build something great together.[27]

This is a tough assignment and a complex one, and it requires expert use of some well-honed power tactics. Growth leaders effectively assess their power bases, foundation on which they stand and they know when and how to use their power sources; otherwise known as transformational command. They understand their organization's *culture*, and they are able to see their organization as a *political system*.

Politics

Politics is another concept that carries negative connotations. Scholar Stephen Robbins (1989) defines organizational politics as "...any behavior by an organizational member that is self-serving." He goes on to say, "It is *functional* when that behavior assists in the attainment of the organizations goals. It is *dysfunctional* when it hinders those goals."[28]

Farrell and Peterson (1982) define organizational political behavior as "...those activities that are not required as part of one's formal role in the organization but that influence, or attempt to influence, the distribution of advantages and disadvantages within the organization."[29]

Researchers have identified certain personality characteristics, needs, and traits that increase the propensity for political behavior. Authoritarian individuals, especially those who take high-risk approaches or who possess an external locus of control, tend to act politically—with less regard for the organization's well-being. Managers and leaders with a high need for power, autonomy, security, or status tend to engage in political behavior.

Certain organizational cultures also promote politicking. Politics is more likely to surface when an organization's resources—or the existing pattern of resources—are declining. Low levels of trust, role ambiguity, and unclear performance evaluation systems foster political activity.

A political perspective can help explain much that seems irrational in organizational life. It can help explain why employees withhold information, restrict output, attempt to "build empires," publicize their successes, hide their failures, distort their achievements, and generally engage in activities that undermine organizational effectiveness.

Differences in thinking and desired goals often bring politics into play. These differences create a tension that must be resolved through political means. This is accomplished in various ways:

- Autocratically ("We'll do it this way.")

- Bureaucratically ("We're supposed to do it this way.")

- Technocratically ("It's best to do it this way.")

- Democratically ("How shall we do it?")

In each case, the choice between alternative paths of action usually hinges on the power relations between the involved actors.

Moreover, people live in the midst of their *interests*—the complex set of goals, values, desires, and expectations that shape their behavior. Interests seen in terms of three interconnected domains:

- *Task* interests—activities related to work responsibilities

- *Career* interests—aspirations and visions about future directions and possibilities

- *Extramural* interests—private attitudes, values, preferences, beliefs, and sets of commitments that lie outside the work domain

The tensions that exist between and among these various interests makes an employee's relation to work inherently *political*—even before taking into account the actions of other organizational members.

In the face of all this organizational complexity, why do growth leaders succeed so well? How do these mid-level managers achieve such impressive organic growth, while operating, for the most part, outside the boundaries of a formal leadership position?

We know from the Carr and others study that these leaders possess some special talents:

- They are rich in experience.

- They are capable of "changing the rules."

- They think like entrepreneurs.

- They embrace new ventures, while managing risk.

- They prefer people to data.

- They practice "pragmatic idealism."

These growth leaders act in morally and emotionally intelligent ways, keeping performance expectations high, while maintaining the good will and allegiance of their people. In describing them, employees use terms such as *caring, motivating,* and *inspiring.*

Growth leaders may also possess a conscious or intuitive understanding of the nature and uses of *power* and the ways in which politics and interests shape individual and organizational behavior. The *political* metaphor helps them to see that organizational goals, structure, technology, job design, leadership style, and other seemingly formal aspects of organizational life all have a *political dimension*—as do the more obvious power plays and conflicts.

Armed with these understandings, growth leaders apply their knowledge and experience in ways that are more creative and in ways that achieve breakout results. Growth leaders possess a sound understanding of their organization's *culture,* and the ways in which a positive, forward-looking culture enhances commitment to organizational goals and increases behavioral consistency. They harness the talents of their teams, and they establish value systems and behavior codes that energize and reward their followers and promote organic growth throughout their organizations.

CHAPTER FIVE

GROWTH LEADERSHIP
AND SOCIAL, EMOTIONAL, MORAL,
AND CULTURAL INTELLIGENCE

G rowth leaders, highly productive mid-managers, consistently maintain the allegiance of their teams, while demanding high performance levels and sustaining a tough-minded approach to complex (and bottom line) issues. These leaders are seen as "tough but fair"—strong-minded and hard-nosed in their approach to problems and opportunities but compassionate in their approach to people. So, what is their secret? How do they crack the growth code and drive team members toward impressive achievements, while eliciting accolades like *caring, inspiring,* and *motivating*?

Growth leaders use well-established strategies and tactics to reach their goals, but they also possess some special characteristics. Researchers Carr and others (2008) tell us that they are rich in experience. Along the way, they have acquired a wide range of skills and a set of diverse experiences—together with a deep-seated belief in their abilities. They value knowledge, and they insist that team members possess needed skill sets—that they expertly exploit. They thrive on challenges, and they look for quick results, while also carefully managing risk. They look to customers and suppliers for ideas, and they deal pragmatically with the organization—they do not fight it.[30]

These growth leaders also may be tapping into some deep-seated "intelligences"— a set of behaviors, attitudes, and personal qualities that shape leadership approaches and fuel business performance. These *social, emotional, moral,* and *cultural* intelligences have proven their worth in recent years—and it is possible that growth leaders are making special use of them. Let us look briefly at each.

Social intelligence

We are all familiar with IQ tests—the tool we use to measure an individual's learning, thinking, and reasoning abilities. When Alfred Binet, a century ago, devised this measure to assess the intelligence of Paris school children, he set off a wave of test creation that has led to the Scholastic Aptitude Test (SAT), American College Test (ACT), Graduation Record Examination (GRE), Miller Analogies Test (MAT), and various other assessment instruments.

Years later, in a 1920 *Harper's Magazine* article, the noted psychologist, Edward L. Thorndike, advanced the view that we possess three kinds of intelligences: abstract, mechanical, and *social* (defined as the ability to understand others and to "act wisely in human relations") Thorndike distinguished between social intelligence and academic ability, but he said little beyond that.

In recent years, Yale researcher Robert Sternberg (1981) has developed a Triarchic view of intelligence—a construct that includes analytical, creative, and practical abilities. Sternberg ties practical intelligence to everyday problem solving, and he explicitly includes *social intelligence*. Professor Sternberg and colleagues have defined some behaviors that reflect social competence:

- Accepts others for what they are

- Admits mistakes

- Displays interest in the world at large

- Keeps appointments—on time

- Possesses a social conscience

- Thinks before speaking and acting

- Displays curiosity

- Avoids snap judgments

- Assesses the relevance of information to problems

- Stays sensitive to other people's needs and desires

- Deals frankly and honestly with self and others

- Displays interest in the immediate environment[31]

Another study, by Kosmitzki and John (1993), showed these central social intelligence dimensions:

- Understands people's thoughts, feelings, and intentions

- Possesses skill in dealing with people

- Understands rules and norms of human relations

- Possesses skill in taking other people's perspectives

- Adapts well in social situations

- Remains warm and caring

- Stays open to new experiences, ideas, and values[32]

In his recent book, *Social Intelligence*, Daniel Goleman (2007) notes that outstanding leadership requires a combination of self-mastery and social intelligence. Self-mastery refers to the ways in which we handle ourselves. It involves qualities of *self-awareness* and *self-control*. In Goleman's words:

> *The leadership competencies that build on self-mastery include a good measure of self-confidence, the drive to improve performance, the ability to stay calm under pressure and to maintain a positive outlook. All these abilities can be seen at full force, for instance, in workers who are outstanding individual performers. The operative word here is* individual— *and that's the rub. When it comes to leaders, effectiveness in relationships makes or breaks. Solo stars are often promoted to leadership positions and then flounder for lack of people skills.*[33]

Social intelligence (although difficult to measure) appears to play a major role in how people intuitively perceive intelligence. Social intelligence specifically geared toward solving the problems of social life. This form of intelligence is a set of skills that helps people manage life tasks, current concerns, and personal projects. This is not evaluated in abstract; only viewed in terms of domains and contexts in which exhibited.

In her essay, "Towards a Feminist Reassessment of Intellectual Virtue," Jane Braaten (1990) uses the phrase *intellectual virtue* to emphasize a teleological social ability—a social ability that leads individuals and communities to certain ends. She argues for a community in which "all members of the community have the opportunity to live well." The construction of such a community, she says, requires special intellectual competence. She calls this competence *social intelligence*, and she identifies six abilities:

- The ability to represent alternative subjective points of view—not merely of a perceptual character but also of an ideological character

- The ability to reason hypothetically about the likely responses of others to courses of events—given all the various subjective points of view

- The ability to recognize social norms and values as socially constructed—not simply made up of *a priori* truths

- The ability to postulate what the social world would be like if it were based on alternative social norms

- The ability to hypothesize about the sources of discord and well-being

- The ability to use all the abilities—and to re-chart intellectual virtue by itself

Professor Braaten argues that social intelligence has the potential, when "unconstrained," to be "not only empowering, but deeply subversive toward coercive, racist, and sexist social structures." Social Intelligence," she says, "has the potential for re-forming our definition of intelligence." She concludes, "If we can learn to value community building as much as we value other abilities, we will create new potentials for living better together."[34]

Some scholars, including Antonio Damasio (2000), argue that Braaten's conceptualization of social intelligence remains incomplete—it does not address the role of emotions and feelings.

Social intelligence, then, is closely related to *emotional intelligence*—a concept that many corporations have integrated into their employee and leadership development programs.

Emotional intelligence

In recent years, the concept of *emotional intelligence* has gained broad acceptance—fueled by the scholarly work of Peter Salovey and John Mayer

(1990) and propelled by Daniel Goleman's (1995) groundbreaking book, *Emotional Intelligence*. Companies around the world have instituted programs that seek to enhance this quality—among all employees—as it's referenced to a core leadership competence.

Mayer and Salovey (the first researchers) have defined emotional intelligence (EI) as "...a type of social intelligence that involves the ability to monitor one's own and others' emotions, to discriminate among them, and to use the information to guide one's thinking and action." They further define it as "...the ability to process emotional information, particularly as it involves the perception, assimilation, understanding, and management of emotion."

In a 1997 publication, scholars Mayer and Salovey identified four branches of EI:

- Emotional perception

- Emotional facilitation of thought

- Emotional understanding

- Emotional management

The four branches stem more from basic psychological processes, to higher and more psychologically integrated processes. The lowest level branch (Branch One), for example, describes the relatively simple abilities of perceiving and expressing emotion. In contrast, the highest-level branch (Branch Four) addresses the conscious, reflective regulation of emotion. Abilities that emerge relatively early in development appear at the top of a given branch. Later developing abilities appear at the bottom.[35]

Branch One: perception, appraisal, and expression of emotion

- Ability to identify emotion in one's physical states, feelings, and thoughts

- Ability to identify emotions in other people through language, sound, appearance, and behavior

- Ability to express emotions accurately and to express needs related to those feelings

- Ability to discriminate between accurate and inaccurate—or honest vs. dishonest—expressions

Branch Two: emotional facilitation of thinking

- Ability to understand that emotions prioritize thinking by directing attention to important information

- Ability to understand that emotions are vivid and available and can be generated as aids to judgment and memory about feelings

- Ability to understand that emotional mood swings can change the individual's perspective from optimistic to pessimistic

- Ability to understand that emotional states differentially encourage specific problem-solving approaches (e.g., when happy feelings facilitate inductive reasoning and creativity)

Branch Three: understanding and analyzing emotions—employing emotional knowledge

- Ability to label emotions and recognize relations between and among the words and the emotions themselves (e.g., the relation between liking and loving)

- Ability to interpret the meanings that emotions convey regarding relationships (e.g., the sadness that often accompanies a loss)

- Ability to understand complex feelings—that is, simultaneous feelings of love and hate, or blends (e.g., awe as a combination of fear and surprise)

- Ability to recognize likely transitions among emotions (e.g., the transition from anger to satisfaction or from anger to shame)

Branch Four: regulation of emotion to promote emotional and intellectual growth

- Ability to stay open to feelings—both pleasant and unpleasant

- Ability to reflectively engage or detach from an emotion, depending on its judged informativeness or utility

- Ability to monitor emotions reflectively in one's self and others (recognizing how clear, typical, influential, or reasonable they are)

- Ability to manage emotion in one's self and others by moderating negative emotions and enhancing pleasant ones, without repressing or exaggerating information they may convey

These traits are elements of emotional intelligence, a high predictor of success—higher, say many researchers, than predictors such as GPA, IQ, and standardized test scores.

Emotional intelligence programs have been around for a while, and their bottom line benefits have been closely studied and well documented. Self-aware, emotionally intelligent leaders create a more positive work climate and relate more effectively to all organizational members. Emotional intelligence, a powerful self-governing tool, closely linked to *moral intelligence*, another self-governing tool, and a powerful leadership competence.

Moral intelligence

Moral intelligence (MQ) has been defined by Jean Piaget as "respect for one's self, and others, as beings with inherent value." Piaget believed that practical morality lies much deeper than one's articulated beliefs and that morality (or mutual respect) is mainly intuitive—not based on analytical, principled reasoning.

Robert Coles (1998), a Harvard social psychiatrist and author of *The Moral Intelligence of Children*, has defined MQ as "…moral behavior tested by life, lived out in the course of our everyday experience."

Authors Doug Lennick and Fred Kiel (2005) define MQ this way:

> *Moral intelligence is the mental capacity to determine how universal human principles should be applied to our values, goals, and actions. In the simplest terms, moral intelligence is the ability to differentiate right from wrong as defined by universal principles. Universal principles are those beliefs about human conduct that are common to all cultures around the world. Thus, we believe they apply to all people, regardless of gender, ethnicity, religious belief, or location on the globe.*[36]

MQ definitions vary, but one reality persists: committed, meaningful, sustained moral action fascinates us and frequently astounds us, and we continue to explore its nature and uses. However, this much we know: the development of sociomoral "maturity" is no simple matter. Even the experts disagree about its nature. The identification-internalization experts emphasize *emotion*; the social learning experts emphasize *behavior*; and the cognitive-developmental experts emphasize *cognition*.

Some researchers are now telling us that these differing emphases have created an artificial trichotomy that has ignored the interplay between and among behavior, thought, and emotion. Moral emotions, they say, cannot occur without some cognitive content; thought always contains some emotional tone (be it cold or hot); and voluntary behavior always possesses an intentional basis. Thus, say these researchers (Walker, Pitts, Hennig, and Matsuba 1995), moral psychology requires a more comprehensive and holistic approach.[37]

In addition, to morally responsible behavior, influenced by many factors—both internal and external to the individual. The scholarly literature surrounding these factors is vast, and social scientists and others continue to debate the definition. Nevertheless, we have identified a few broad moral dimensions:

- Morality includes the ability to distinguish between good and bad—and the motivation to choose well.

- Morality includes a sense of obligation toward standards shared by a social collective.

- Morality includes a concern for the welfare of others—a concern that possesses both a cognitive and an affective component that carries implications for judgment and conduct, and that involves obligations beyond an individual's unmitigated selfish desires.

- Morality includes the responsibility for acting on one's concern for others— expressed through acts of caring, benevolence, kindness, and mercy.

- Morality includes a concern for the rights of others—a concern that includes a sense of justice and a commitment to the fair resolution of conflicts.

- Morality includes a commitment to honesty in interpersonal dealings.

Moral identity has been defined as a "self-conception organized around a set of moral traits." Researchers who have studied moral exemplars say that they possess a "moral center"—a moral core that lies at the center of their selves.

They exhibit a unity between self and morality, and they possess a destiny that largely defines moral goals.

For moral exemplars, morality is a core construct in the maintenance of their identity and self-evaluation; it is relevant to the deepest sense of who they are. In their examination of twenty-three moral exemplars, researchers Colby and Damon (2006) determined that exemplars in general achieve not only moral understanding but also "ever greater moral clarity"—a kind of independence in moral perception. Their vision remains realistic, and they remain rigorously truthful, steadfastly resisting distortion and illusory interpretations of events. They avoid grandiose biases, misrepresentations, and cognitive distortions (e.g., minimizing, mislabeling, blaming). Furthermore, they link mature and true moral perception to action.[38]

Few among us will attain moral exemplar status, but we all possess the capacity for increasing our mature moral judgment—and for building a solid working moral intelligence.

It is difficult to quantify the business advantages of morally intelligent leadership, but we see clearly the business costs of *moral ignorance*. More than 70 percent of American consumers have, at some point, punished companies for unethical behavior—by either avoiding their products or directly criticizing the company.

Morally intelligent leaders inspire and motivate their people. They help establish a company's moral authority—a solid base on which to build effective formal authority systems and a creative corporate climate. A sound moral intelligence, resting on a strong moral identity, provides the motivation for sustained, committed moral action. This moral intelligence helps us define the parameters of moral conduct and helps us identify our horizons of significance. For some people (not all), it is linked to *cultural intelligence*—an ability to deal effectively with cultural diversity.

Cultural intelligence

Cultural intelligence (CQ), broadly defined, consists of the ability to deal effectively with cultural diversity. Culturally intelligent individuals understand that the world is really a *set* of worlds within worlds—each with a distinctive set of values, beliefs, attitudes, and expectations (in short, a distinctive culture). Cultural intelligence picks up where emotional intelligence leaves off. It allows individuals to distinguish between behaviors produced by a specific culture and those peculiar to a specific individual or those found in all humans. The two intelligences, however, share a common critical element. That is a propensity to suspend judgment—to think before acting.

Researchers P. Christopher Earley and Elaine Mosakowski (2004) have developed six CQ profiles that distinguish levels of cultural intelligence:

- *Provincials* work well with people of similar background—but run into trouble when venturing farther afield.

- *Analysts* methodically use elaborate learning strategies to decipher a foreign culture's rules and expectations. Analysts quickly understand that they are in foreign territory but then ascertain, usually in stages, the nature of the patterns at work and how they should interact with them.

- *Naturals* rely on intuition and first impressions, rather than on a systematic learning style. When faced with ambiguous multicultural circumstances, Naturals sometimes falter.

- *Ambassadors* may know little about the culture they have entered, but they quickly convince others that they belong. Ambassadors observe how others have succeeded, and they exude confidence.

- *Mimics* possess a high degree of control over their actions and behaviors. They put hosts and guests at ease, facilitate communication, and build trust.

- *Chameleons* possess all the CQ sources—head, body, heart—and (unlike most newcomers to organizational or national cultures) generate few ripples.[39]

Why do some individuals function effectively in new cultures and among "strangers" and others falter? High (at least adequate) social, emotional, and moral quotients by themselves do not guarantee success. Anecdotal and empirical evidence shows that individuals with high cultural intelligence—either innate or cultivated—will more effectively comprehend their circumstances and choose the right actions.

Growth leaders possess solid business skills, and their success depends on various factors—a good product or service, a favorable business climate, a supportive organization. Leaders imbued with social, emotional, moral, and cultural intelligences may also possess the potential for moving leadership effectiveness to the next level. These "quiet leaders"—staying always sensitive to followers' needs—are capable of inspiring high performance and trust. They are guided by a common set of principles—a set of intelligences (social, emotional, moral, and cultural) that support their leadership activities.

CONCLUSION

The recent focus on growth leadership has been fueled by a dynamic and shifting commercial environment and by ongoing changes in organizational structures. Consider the trends.

Many businesses are now multinational organizations—global in nature and led by a collective set of thought processes. Time and space mean little to a global company, and neither do borders and geographical location. Global companies operate seamlessly around the world in a 24/7 environment—leveraging technology, global networks, and best practices. Leaders (at all levels) are now required to "think globally" while "acting locally"—a key to continued growth. They must find ways to bring together dissimilar employees from disparate cultures, while maintaining the uniqueness of local identities.

Moreover, advancing technology is radically changing the business landscape. Much of the "new work" has been inspired by advances in communications technology—the desktop computer, the internet, wireless broadband, hand-held mobile devices, and conferencing software. The explosion in these new technologies—together with the seemingly endless potentials for their use—is outstripping and sometimes undermining work structures that have endured for over a century.

New organizational structures are evolving to meet the new competitive challenges—less hierarchical in nature and more functionally split than traditional bureaucratic organizations. These new organizations may possess stable structures—a core structure that is relatively static—but may have a more fluid support structure, drawing on resources from within and outside the firm.

In the face of these challenges, economic crisis, and myriad others, companies are looking increasingly to their mid-level managers for creative and effective leadership. Many of these growth leaders are delivering breakout results. They are setting visions, while maintaining a focus on strategic and tactical thinking. They are driving innovation, while operating pragmatically and keeping an eye always on the bottom line. They are achieving organic growth, while minimizing risk and fostering organizational cohesion and stability.

Furthermore, they are leapfrogging the competition—not because they are doing everything better, but because they are concentrating on developing the right operational levers.

I hope this book will further stimulate thinking about the nature of growth leadership, and that the information will help others understand and further exploit the growth leadership potentials within their respective organizations.

> To lead people, walk beside them…. As for the best leaders, the people do not notice their existence. The next best, the people honor and praise. The next, the people fear; and the next the people hate…. When the best leader's work is done the people say, "We did it ourselves." (Lao-tsu, 6th century B.C. sage)

ACKNOWLEDGEMENTS

No book about leadership gets written without its own obligations. First, I wish to thank Stephen N. Barton, MD, PhD, who encouraged me to develop the book and who was supportive throughout the project. Secondly, I would like to thank Orlo Otteson for his research and editing contributions, including insuring that all citations, credits were correct. For this, I am grateful. Thirdly, to all the leaders in my personal and professional life from boyhood to the present who have shown me the value of effective leadership; I dedicate this book to my dad, my mom, WT, Brenda, and Stephanie.

I'm also indebted to Eric, Tim, Andy, Stan, Malinda, Chris, Alex, Jeff (Pump Station) Walker, Phil Rautine, Sonny Yarbrough, Vernon Matlock, Stacy Nelson, Bud Grimes, Elwood & Carolyn Doss, Timm Jonson, Doc & Jo Cole, Scott S and David W, the late Bob Ritz, Tina & Teresa, Dennis & Courtney, Larry Masters, Carol Long, late Dr. Bob Walker, Garry Anderson, Dr. Ken Carter, Jacob Edwards, Carolyn Edwards, Tim Smith, Harley D. Fergusun Jr., Mitch Milam, the late Mr. Lipscomb, Dustin M & Randy W, the late Mrs. Couch, the great Brad Fellows, Allen Steele, Tom B & Steve A, Mickey Smith, Mbenga, late Christie Walker, Chrystal & Heather, Sammy Trimm, Bri, "Tony, Heather,& Dave," Donte, Richard Albright, D Thompson, Bobby Seals, Jimmy Hicks, Peter Lowe, the late Jack Alison, Larry Triplet, Harry and Joy, John Ritz, the late Marvin Rodgers & Howard Lee, Bruce (Dr. Phil) Wittenberg, Mark & Bridget, Ben Bostrom, Min Kao, Ed Jolly, Bruce Greason & Gloria Eldridge, David Plouffe, Michael Brantley, "S.C.," Jay McKinley, Moungi, Coach Pete Billingsley, Bill Rhodes, Jeffrey-John-Jamie, Ron and Rob, Alex Pitsos, Jeremy Stump, Robert Baim, Dax, S Shreve, Naomi, John Updike, Kevin Yochum, Dusty Brighton & family, Dr. Whitney, Dr. Lynn W. Conrad, David Fritz, and the Walters family.

And those from the classroom who taught me about true living, specifically Bunny Creasman, Steve Camp, Mel Albright, Dougal Moore, Terry Wisby, Eloise Pereira, Barbara Hayes, Debra Coffee, Ann Edens, Mike Pappas, Mark Emery, Coach Taylor, Tom Schmidt, Nancy Austin, Dr. Victoria Sitter, and Dr. Bruce Montgomery.

My biggest debt is to Java Café, EFC, Vanderbilt, Scooters, B.U.M.C, C.A.K. Class of 1990, UTM Class of 1994, Alpha Kappa Psi, OCCTC, CLC, my DSCC students, Kellwood, Milligan Cohort B-2006, and most of all my entire Microsoft family!

INTRODUCTION:

1. Sean D. Carr et al., "In Search of Growth Leaders," *MIT Sloan Management Review* 49, no. 4 (2008).

2. Charles Handy, "The New Language of Organizing and Its Implications for Leaders," in *The Leaders of the Future*, ed. Frances Hesselbein, Marshall Goldsmith, and Richard Beckhard (San Francisco, CA: Jossey-Bass, 1997), 6-7.

CHAPTER 1:

3. Ronald Chernow, *Titan: the Life of John D. Rockefeller, Sr.* (New York: Vintage, 1997), 182.

4. Richard Florida, *The Rise of the Creative Class. And How It's Affecting Work, Leisure, Community and Everyday Life* (New York: Basic Books, 2002), 56.

5. William James, "William James on Exceptional Mental States: The 1896 Lowell Lectures," quoted in Madelle Becker, "Nineteenth Century Foundations of Creativity Research," *Creativity Research Journal*, 8 (1995): 222.

6. William James, *Talks to Teachers on Psychology* (New York: Henry Holt, 1908), 64.

7. James M. Kouzes and Barry Z. Posner, *The Leadership Challenge* (San Francisco: Jossey-Bass, 1995).

8. Sean D. Carr et al., "In Search of Growth Leaders," *MIT Sloan Management Review* 49, no. 4 (2008).

9. Michael Kirton, *Adaptors and Innovators: Styles of Creativity and Problem Solving* (Berkhamsted, UK: Occupational Research Center, 1999).

10. R.M. Burnside, Teresa Amabile, and S. S. Gryskiewicz, "Assessing Organizational Climates for Creativity and Innovation: Methodological Review of Large Company Audits," in *New Directions in Creative and Innovative Management*, ed. Yuji Ijiri and Robert Kuhn (Cambridge, MA: Ballinger, 1988), 169-185.

11. Peter G. Northouse, *Leadership: Theory and Practice*, 3rd ed. (Thousand Oaks, CA: Sage, 2004), 177.

12. Dean K. Simonton, *Genius, Creativity and Leadership* (Cambridge, MA: Harvard University Press, 1984), 181.

13. Charles Handy, *Understanding Organizations: How the Way Organizations Actually Work Can Be Used to Manage Them Better* (New York: Oxford University Press, 1993).

CHAPTER 2:

14. Warren Bennis and Burt Nanus, *Leaders: Strategies for Taking Charge* (New York: Harper & Row, 1985), 112.

15. James Collins and Jerry Porras, *Built to Last: Successful Habits of Visionary Companies* (New York: Harper Business, 1994), 94.

16. Scott Isaksen and Donald Treffinger, *Creative Problem Solving: The Basic Course* (Buffalo, NY: Bearly Limited, 1985).

17. Donald Treffinger, Scott Isaksen, and Roger Firestien, *Handbook of Creative Learning, Volume 1* (Williamsville, NY: Center for Creative Learning, 1982).

18. Gerard Puccio, Mary Murdock, and Marie Mance, *Creative Leadership: Skills That Drive Change* (Thousand Oaks, CA: Sage Publications, 2007), 87-107.

19. Hunter Lewis, *A Question of Values* (New York: HarperCollins, 1990), 5-20.

20. James Kouzes and Barry Posner, *The Leadership Challenge: How to Keep Getting Extraordinary Things Done in Organizations* (San Francisco: Jossey-Bass, 1995), 98.

CHAPTER 3:

21. Eileen Jay and David Perkins, *Problem finding: The Search for Mechanisms*. In *Creativity Research Handbook, Volume 1*, ed. M. A. Runco (Creskill, NJ: Hampton, 1997), 259.

22. Gerard Puccio, and Mary Murdock, and Marie Mance, *Creative Leadership: Skills That Drive Change* (Thousand Oaks, CA: Sage Publications, 2007), 168.

CHAPTER 4:

23. Thomas Peters and Robert Waterman, *In Search of Excellence* (New York: Warner Books, 1984) 82-3.

24. Phillip Selznick, *Leadership and Administration* (New York: McGraw-Hill, 1982), 42.

25. Paul Hersey and Kenneth Blanchard, *Management of Organizational Behavior* (Englewood Cliffs, NJ: Prentice-Hall, 1982).

26. Lester Bittel and Jackson Ramsey, *Handbook for Professional Managers* (New York: McGraw-Hill, 1985).

27. Sean D. Carr et al., "In Search of Growth Leaders," *MIT Sloan Management Review* 49 (2008).

28. Stephen Robbins, *Organizational Behavior: Concepts, Controversies, and Applications* (Englewood Cliffs, NJ: Prentice-Hall, 1989), 353.

29. Dan Farrell and James Peterson, "Patterns of Political Behavior in Organizations," *Academy of Management Review*, 7, no. 3 (1982): 403-12.

CHAPTER 5:

30. Sean D. Carr et al., "In Search of Growth Leaders," *MIT Sloan Management Review* 49, no. 4 (2008).

31. Robert Sternberg et al., "People's Conceptions of Intelligence, *Journal of Personality & Social Psychology* 41 (1981): 37-55.

32. C. Kosmitzki and O. P. John, "The Implicit Use of Explicit Conceptions of Social Intelligence," *Personality & Individual Differences* 15 (1993): 11-23.

33. Daniel Goleman, *Social Intelligence* (New York: Bantam Dell Pub Group, 2007).

34. Jane Braaten, "Towards a Feminist Reassessment of Intellectual Virtue," *Hypatia* (Fall 1990).

35. John Mayer and Peter Salovey, *Emotional Development and Emotional Intelligence: Educational Implications* (New York: Basic Books, 1997), 10-11.

36. Doug Lennick and Fred Kiel, *Moral Intelligence: Enhancing Business Performance & Leadership Success* (Upper Saddle River, NJ: Wharton School Publishing, 2005), xxxiii.

37. Melanie Killen and Daniel Hart, *Morality in Everyday Life: Developmental Perspectives* (New York: Cambridge University Press, 1995), 371-407.

38. Killen and Hart, 342-70.

39. P. Christopher Earley and Elaine Mosakowski, "Cultural Intelligence," *Harvard Business Review* (October 2004): 139-46.